Intro Workbook
ACTIVE
Skills for Communication

Chuck Sandy • Curtis Kelly

Series Consultant:
Neil J. Anderson

Australia • Brazil • Japan • Korea • Mexico • Singapore • Spain • United Kingdom • United States

ACTIVE Skills for Communication, Workbook Intro
Sandy / Kelly / Anderson

Publisher: Andrew Robinson
Editorial Manager: Sean Bermingham
Senior Development Editor: Ian Purdon
Associate Development Editor: Lauren Rodan
Director of Global Marketing: Ian Martin
Content Project Manager: Tan Jin Hock
Senior Print Buyer: Mary Beth Hennebury
Editorial Project Management: Content*Ed Publishing Solutions, LLC
Compositor / Cover Designer: Chrome Media Group / C. Hanzie / M. Chong

Photo Credits

Shutterstock: pages 4, 5 (all except top row right and second row left), 6, 7 (all except top row left), 8 (top row right and bottom row left and right), 9 (top row), 10 (all except bottom row left), 11, 12 (all except top row left and right and bottom row right), 14, 15, 18, 19 (bottom), 21, 22, 23, 24 (top), 25, 26 (all except bottom row right), 27, 28, 29, 33, 34, 35, 36, 38, 40 (all except bottom right), 41, 42 (bottom), 43, 46, 47, 48, 49, 50 (all except bottom row center right), 51, 52, 53, 54 (top row left and bottom), 55, 56 (bottom), 57 (bottom); iStockphoto: pages 5 (top row right and second row left), 7 (top row left), 8 (top row left and center and bottom row center), 9 (second row and bottom), 10 (bottom row left), 12 (top row left and right and bottom row right), 19 (top), 20, 24 (bottom), 26 (bottom row right), 37, 39, 40 (bottom right), 50 (bottom row center right), 54 (top row center and right), 56 (top); Landov: page 42 (top); Photos.com: page 57 (top and center)

Copyright © 2010 Heinle, Cengage Learning

ALL RIGHTS RESERVED. No part of this work covered by the copyright herein may be reproduced, transmitted, stored or used in any form or by any means graphic, electronic, or mechanical, including but not limited to photocopying, recording, scanning, digitizing, taping, Web distribution, information networks, or information storage and retrieval systems, except as permitted under Section 107 or 108 of the 1976 United States Copyright Act, without the prior written permission of the publisher.

For permission to use material from this text or product, submit all requests online at **www.cengage.com/permissions**
Further permissions questions can be emailed to **permissionrequest@cengage.com**

ISBN-13: 978-1-4240-0110-1
ISBN-10: 1-4240-0110-2

Heinle
20 Channel Center Street
Boston, Massachusetts 02210
USA

Cengage Learning is a leading provider of customized learning solutions with office locations around the globe, including Singapore, the United Kingdom, Australia, Mexico, Brazil, and Japan. Locate our local office at:
international.cengage.com/region

Cengage Learning products are represented in Canada by Nelson Education, Ltd.

Visit Heinle online at **elt.heinle.com**
Visit our corporate website at **www.cengage.com**

Printed in the United States of America
1 2 3 4 5 6 7 8 9 10   13 12 11 10 09

Contents

Unit 1: Personal Poster 4

Unit 2: Our Favorites 8

Unit 3: Design a Town 12

Review 1 16

Unit 4: What's for Dinner? 18

Unit 5: Every Day's a Holiday 22

Unit 6: The Everyday Hero Award 26

Review 2 30

Unit 7: Now Hiring 32

Unit 8: Family Ties 36

Unit 9: Timeline 40

Review 3 44

Unit 10: An Amazing Trip 46

Unit 11: Computer Dating Service 50

Unit 12: Talent Show 54

Review 4 58

Progress Check 1 60

Progress Check 2 61

Progress Check 3 62

Progress Check 4 63

Personal Poster   1

Working on Vocabulary

A Write. Look at the photo and read the information. Complete the forms for the people.

Marissa (Machan) Silva, Sao Paulo, Brazil

Jon (Jojo) Lee, Seoul, Korea

First name (1) __Marissa__
Last name (2) _____
Nickname (3) _____
Hometown (4) _____

First name (5) _____
Last name (6) _____
Nickname (7) _____
Hometown (8) _____

B Number. Number the sentences in the correct order to make a conversation.

a. ____ Sure, Machan. What's this?
b. ____ Hi, Jon. I'm Marissa Silva.
c. ____ Sure, Jojo. Please call me Machan.
d. ____ Call me Jojo. All my friends do.
e. ____ It's a map of Brazil. I'm from Sao Paulo.
f. __1__ Hi. I'm Jon Lee.

C Write. Write the correct sentence under each photo.

Mari is really fashionable.
~~Vanessa is very athletic.~~
Michael looks very shy.
Pat looks really friendly.

   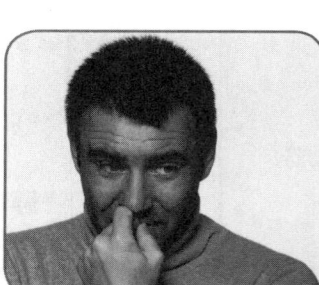

Vanessa is very athletic.

Working on Grammar

A Write. Complete the conversations with *What's this?*, *What are these?*, or *Who's this?*

1. **A:** What's this?
   B: It's my new cell phone. I love it.

2. **A:** _____
   B: She's my best friend, Sally. She's cool.

3. **A:** _____
   B: They're coffee beans. I work in a café.

4. **A:** _____
   B: It's the Oriental Pearl TV Tower. It's in Shanghai.

5. **A:** _____
   B: He's my history teacher. He's nice.

6. **A:** _____
   B: They're drums. I take lessons.

B Circle. Circle the correct words to complete the Internet greeting card.

Hi Mark!
How are you? **(1)** *This is* / *These are* my new headphones. **(2)** *It's* / *they're* fantastic. I'm a DJ at the KittyKat Club now. **(3)** *It's* / *They're* a lot of fun. The manager's name is Frankie. **(4)** *He's* / *It's* really nice. Frankie plays in a band called "The Frankies." **(5)** *It's* / *They're* really good. I DJ every night so come by!

Personal Poster 5

Working on Fluency

A Check [✓]. Check the best response for each statement.

1. **A:** Someday I want to get a pilot's license.
   B: __✓__ Oh really? Why?   _____ Yes, I think so, too
   A: _I love airplanes and air travel._

2. **A:** Someday I want to learn how to speak French.
   B: _____ Well, I don't know.   _____ Why French?
   A: _____

3. **A:** Patrick looks really cool.
   B: _____ Yes, I think so, too.   _____ Oh really? That's nice.
   A: _____

4. **A:** This is my favorite store. I love shopping.
   B: _____ Hmm. I see. Why?   _____ Yeah, really.
   A: _____

B Number. Decide which sentence best completes each conversation in activity A. Write the number. Then add the sentences to the conversations.

_____ I love his leather jacket.   _____ I want to live in Paris someday.
__1__ I love airplanes and air travel.   _____ I like kids and I like teaching.
_____ Let's go to Eastwood Shopping Center this weekend.

C Write. Complete the conversations with your own ideas.

1. **You:** What's this?
   Friend: It's a tennis racket. I think tennis is great.
   You: _____

2. **You:** What are these?
   Friend: They're books. Reading is really fun.
   You: _____

3. **You:** Who's this?
   Friend: It's Madonna. She's cool.
   You: _____

4. **You:** What's this?
   Friend: It's a picture of New York.
   You: _____

Critical Thinking

> Use the information you have to guess about people.

A Check [✓]. Check the sentences you would use for someone you don't know well.

1. _____ Jon looks really friendly.   _____ Jon is friendly.
2. _____ Sara is really athletic.   _____ Sara looks really athletic.
3. _____ Leticia looks really shy.   _____ Leticia is really shy.
4. _____ Carlos is very fashionable.   _____ Carlos looks very fashionable.

B Write. Look at each of these people and read about them. Then write sentences with *is* or *looks* to describe them. Use the words below or ideas of your own.

> athletic   cool   easy-going   fashionable   friendly   shy

1. Carla is your new classmate. She sits in the back of the room. She never talks or smiles.
   Carla looks shy.

2. Peter is your best friend. He plays soccer and tennis. He loves playing sports.

3. Jun is a new teacher at school. He always smiles and says hello.

4. Yoko is your sister. She plays in a band and has many friends.

5. Mrs. Mitchell is your mother's friend. She loves designer shops. She always wears nice clothes and shoes.

6. Mark is a new member at the gym. You sometimes talk to him but you don't know him well.

Our Favorites 2

Working on Vocabulary

A Check [✓]. Check the things you like. Then, write your favorite kind for each thing you checked.

1. ✓ ice cream
   strawberry

2. ☐ pizza

3. ☐ soda

4. ☐ music

5. ☐ movies

6. ☐ sports

B Match. Draw lines to match the category on the left with the matching item on the right.

1. morning drink ○ — ○ a. fruit salad
2. holiday ○   ○ b. black coffee
3. singer ○   ○ c. kangaroo
4. movie star ○   ○ d. Avril Lavigne
5. animal ○   ○ e. Brad Pitt
6. food ○   ○ f. Christmas

C Circle. Circle the word that does not belong.

1. karaoke   pop music   singer   (actor)
2. tennis   basketball   team   soccer
3. mall   store   online   weekend
4. winter   morning   summer   autumn
5. English   homework   math   science

8 Unit 2

Working on Grammar

A Write. Write questions. Then answer with statements from the box that are true for you.

> Yes, I do. I'm crazy about it.   Yes. I like it.   It's OK.
> No, I don't like it very much.   I can't stand it.

1. Q: <u>Do you like movies?</u>   2. Q: _____   3. Q: _____
   A: <u>No, I can't stand movies.</u>   A: _____   A: _____

4. Q: _____   5. Q: _____   6. Q: _____
   A: _____   A: _____   A: _____

B Write. Complete the interview with information that's true for you.

Interviewer: Hi. May I ask you a few questions?
You: <u>Sure. Go ahead.</u>
Interviewer: Do you like eating at restaurants?
You: _____
Interviewer: What's your favorite restaurant?
You: _____
Interviewer: How about fast food? Do you like it?
You: _____
Interviewer: What's your favorite fast food?
You: _____
Interviewer: Thank you very much. Have a nice day!

C Circle. Circle the correct word.

1. *What's* / *Who's* your favorite actor?
2. *What's* / *Who's* your favorite color?
3. *When* / *Where* is your favorite time of day?
4. *What's* / *Who's* your favorite song?

Our Favorites

Working on Fluency

A Check [✓]. Check the best response.

1. I really like music from the 1960s.
   - [✓] That's unusual.
   - [ ] Me neither.

2. I can't stand winter.
   - [ ] Not me. It's too cold.
   - [ ] Really? It's my favorite season.

3. I really like my hometown.
   - [ ] Not me. I can't stand my hometown.
   - [ ] Me neither. It's boring.

4. I'm crazy about instant noodles.
   - [ ] That's interesting.
   - [ ] Really? Why not?

5. I don't like shopping very much.
   - [ ] Really? I'm crazy about it.
   - [ ] Well, not really.

6. I'm crazy about doing homework.
   - [ ] Hmm. I see. That's interesting.
   - [ ] Oh, really? Me neither.

B Write. Complete the conversations with *me too*, *not me*, or *me neither* so they are true for you. Then add more information.

1. I'm crazy about coffee. How about you?
   Not me. I can't stand it.

2. I really like dancing. How about you?
   _____

3. I like going to karaoke. How about you?
   _____

4. I don't like reading very much.
   _____

5. I'm crazy about cooking.
   _____

6. I can't stand watching sports.
   _____

C Number. Number the sentences in the correct order to make a conversation.

a. ____ Marie: I'm crazy about hip hop.
b. ____ Marie: I really like Kanye West. How about you?
c. _1_ Joe: What's your favorite kind of music?
d. ____ Joe: He's OK but I don't like him very much.
e. ____ Joe: Really? Me too. Who's your favorite singer?

Critical Thinking

> Think about language that makes responses nicer or more polite.

A Check [✓]. Check the nicer response in each conversation.

1. I'm crazy about playing chess.
   - ☐ Really? I can't stand it.
   - ☑ That's interesting.

2. I like studying history. Do you like it?
   - ☐ No, I don't. I don't like history at all.
   - ☐ That's unusual. What kind of history?

3. I'm a morning person! It's my favorite time of day.
   - ☐ Hmm. I see. That's nice but I'm a night person.
   - ☐ Not me! I'm a night person.

4. I don't listen to music. I don't like it very much.
   - ☐ What? Why not?
   - ☐ Oh really? That's unusual. I love music.

5. I'm crazy about comic books. I like Batman.
   - ☐ Really? You're kidding, right?
   - ☐ Hmm. I see. That's nice.

B Read and check [✓]. Read this email from your new roommate and the two replies below. Then check the reply that is more polite.

From: JLee@ASC.com
To: Carlos Barbola
Subject: Your New Roommate

Hi! My name is Jason Lee. Call me Jason. I'm your new roommate! Let me tell you about myself. I'm crazy about board games. Also, I like chess and I really like playing card games, too. How about you? I love heavy metal music. My favorite band is Metallica. What's your favorite kind of music?

See you soon! ~Jason

☐ Hi Jason. So you're my new roommate? That's interesting. Let me tell you about myself. I can't stand board games and I hate chess. My favorite kind of music is classical music. Do you like classical music? I think maybe you hate it. That's OK. See you soon.

☐ Hi Jason. Thanks for your email. Let me tell you about myself. I'm crazy about classical music. I don't like heavy metal very much, but it's OK. I like playing cards, but I don't like chess very much. Someday I want to learn how to play chess. Can you teach me? See you soon.

C Underline. Why is the reply you checked more polite? Underline the polite words and sentences.

Design a Town 3

Working on Vocabulary

A Write. Look at the photo clues. Complete the crossword puzzle.

Across

Down

B Check [✓]. Check the place that is different.

1. ☐ school   ☐ train station   ✓ park   ☐ store
2. ☐ lake   ☐ river   ☐ mountain   ☐ bridge
3. ☐ fast food restaurant ☐ pizza place ☐ DVD rental shop   ☐ coffee shop
4. ☐ fitness center ☐ clothing store   ☐ CD shop   ☐ convenience store
5. ☐ hotel   ☐ bank   ☐ house   ☐ apartment
6. ☐ movie theater ☐ office   ☐ fitness center   ☐ game center

12 Unit 3

Working on Grammar

A Circle. Look at the picture. Then circle the correct words to complete the sentences.

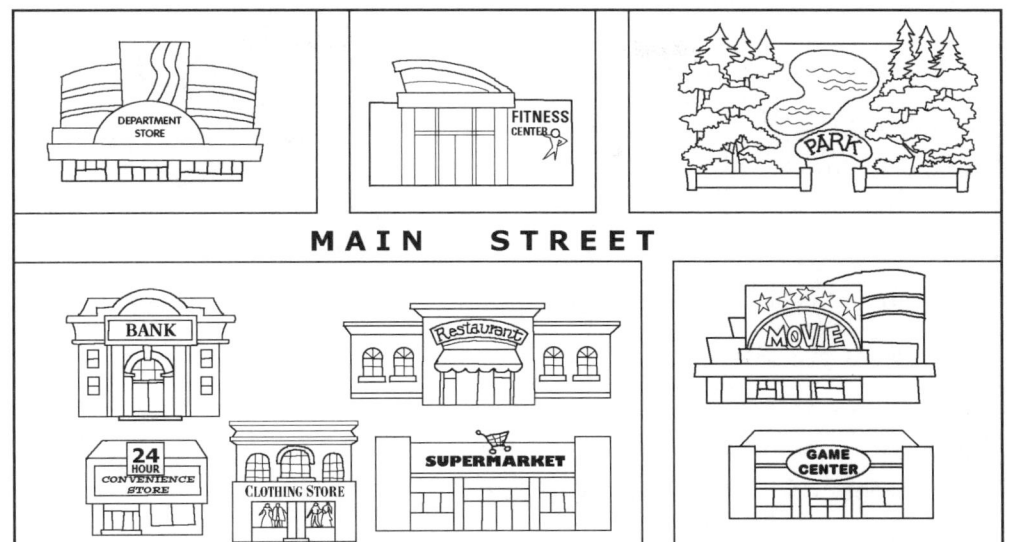

1. There's a bank *across from* / *next to* the department store.
2. The fitness center is *next to* / *across from* the bank.
3. There are trees *in* / *in front of* the park.
4. The restaurant is *between* / *behind* the bank and the movie theater.
5. There's a convenience store *behind* / *in front of* the bank.
6. There *are* / *aren't* any cars on the street.

B Write. Look at the picture again and write sentences using *in*, *across from*, *in front of*, or *next to*.

1. fitness center / the restaurant — There's a fitness center across from the restaurant.
2. department store / bank _____
3. game center / movie theater _____
4. supermarket / clothing store _____
5. trees / park _____

C Draw. Draw simple pictures of these sentences.

1. There are some mountains behind the town.
2. There's a bridge over the river.
3. There are some trees in front of the house.

Design a Town 13

Working on Fluency

A Write. Write questions to confirm the information and complete the conversations.

1. **Marta:** Let's meet at the fitness center.
   Steve: <u>The fitness center?</u>
   Marta: Yes. It's across from the restaurant.
2. **Julia:** There's a great restaurant next to the movie theater.
   Daisuke: _____
   Julia: Uh huh. This restaurant is next to the movie theater, not across from it.
3. **Pedro:** Let's meet at 7 p.m.
   Mike: _____
   Pedro: Yes, at 7 p.m. Our class starts at 7:15.
4. **Ray:** Let's meet at the sports center at 2:00.
   Mimi: _____
   Ray: That's right. Marco has a big game there at 3:00.

B Number. Number the sentences in the correct order to make a conversation.

a. ____ **Jill:** The river? That's nice. What else can you see?
b. ____ **Amy:** No, I can't see them from my window, but I can see the river.
c. _1_ **Jill:** Are there any mountains near your home?
d. ____ **Amy:** There's a small bridge over the river. I can see that too.
e. ____ **Jill:** Can you see the mountains from your bedroom window?
f. ____ **Amy:** Yes, there are. There are some mountains behind my house.

C Write. Answer these questions about the place where you live.

1. What things are there near your home?
   _____

2. What things are there near your school?
   _____

3. What things are there between your home and your school?
   _____

4. What stores are there in your town?
   _____

Critical Thinking

Think about how follow-up questions work and why people ask them.

A Read and check [✓]. Read the conversations. Check the best question.

1. **A:** The next train? Let's see. It leaves in two minutes.
   B: [✓] In two minutes?   [ ] The train?
   A: Yes, that's right. Here's your ticket. Hurry!

2. **A:** Do you like this bag? It's $1,000.
   B: [ ] $1,000? You're kidding.   [ ] The bag? Hmmm. I see.
   A: No, I'm not. It's $1,000. Would you like to buy it, sir?

3. **A:** The bank is across from post office, next to George's.
   B: [ ] George's? Is it a store?   [ ] The bank? Where?
   A: No, It's a café. Try it! It's our city's best restaurant.

4. **A:** Hey Mari! My birthday is today. I'm 21 now.
   B: [ ] Today? Really? Happy Birthday.   [ ] Now? What time is it?
   A: Thank you very much!

5. **A:** That's seven dollars and seventeen cents, please.
   B: [ ] Seventy cents?   [ ] Please?
   A: No, seventeen cents.

B Write. Why does speaker B in each conversation in activity A repeat something? Choose the reason. Write the letter of the reason next to each conversation number.

a. The speaker is surprised or shocked
b. The speaker needs more information.
c. The speaker wants to check his or her listening.

1. _____   2. _____   3. _____   4. _____   5. _____

C Think and check [✓]. Think about each conversation again. Check the situations in which speaker A is probably a stranger. How do you know?

1. _____   2. _____   3. _____   4. _____   5. _____

Design a Town

Review 1 — Units 1–3

A Write. Read the clues and complete the crossword puzzle.

Across
4. Someone in a movie
6. The opposite of "boring"
8. The place you are from
10. A sporty person is _____.
11. Fast food _____
13. Item often found over a river
14. The place sick people go
16. Short for popular music
18. You take classes at _____.
19. _____ store

Down
1. The language of France
2. Your family name
3. An animal from Australia
5. Ice _____ cone
7. Quiet and _____
9. The last season of the year
12. Where you buy food
14. Use these to listen to music.
15. Time period between morning and night
17. Fitness _____

B Draw and write. Make a postcard. Draw a map of the area around your home. Show your home and three other places. Write sentences to describe your map.

Your map:

Dear _____,
Hello from _____.
This is where I live. My home is
_____.
There is a _____ near here.
There are _____ in the area, too. There _____.
It's a _____ place. Please visit me!
Yours,
_____

C Number. Rey and Yumi are doing the Challenge from Unit 1 in the Student Book. Match these phrases with the phrases in **bold** that have the same meaning. Write the numbers.

a. _____ not very much
b. _____ my name is
c. _____ Oh really?
d. _____ So do I
e. _____ you can
f. _____ I'm glad to
g. _____ around
h. _____ I'm crazy about

Rey: Hi. **(1) I'm** Reynaldo Diaz.
Yumi: Hi, Reynaldo. I'm Yumi Ito.
Rey: **(2) It's nice to** meet you. **(3) Please** call me Rey.
Yumi: Call me Yumi. All my friends do.
Rey: OK, Yumi. Please tell me about your poster. What's this?
Yumi: It's my hometown. I'm from Tokyo.
Rey: **(4) That's interesting.** Where in Tokyo?
Yumi: I live **(5) near** Diamon Station. I can see Tokyo Tower from my house.
Rey: Wow. That's cool. What are these?
Yumi: They're CDs. **(6) I love** music.
Rey: **(7) Me, too.** Who's your favorite singer?
Yumi: I really like Celine Dion. Do you like her, too?
Rey: **(8) Not really**, but she's OK.

D Research and write. Choose your favorite singer or actor. Use the Internet to find out more. Paste or draw a picture of the person in the chart and answer the questions.

Name of singer or actor: _____ (Draw or paste picture here.)	Birthday: _____ Hometown: _____ Hobbies: _____ _____ Favorites: _____ _____ Other information: _____ _____ _____

What's for Dinner? 4

Working on Vocabulary

A Write. Write the food words below in the correct columns. Then add one more item to each list.

> cabbage   chicken   rice   milk   ~~cherries~~
> pumpkin   flour   beef   lettuce   bananas
> ham   cheese   onions   bread   butter

cherries _____   _____   _____   _____

B Match. Write *a bag of, a box of,* or *a bottle of* for each item.

1. _____ cereal
2. _____ soda
3. _____ cooking oil
4. _____ flour
5. _____ chocolates
6. _____ rice

C Write. What do you need to make these dishes? Write three or more items. Use your own ideas or items from activities A and B.

1. **An American Pumpkin Pie**

2. **Your Favorite Sandwich**

18   Unit 4

Working on Grammar

A Circle. Circle the correct words to complete the conversation.

1. Hey, *(is)* / *are* there any whole wheat bread?
   Yes, *there's* / *there are* a loaf of it in the kitchen.
2. How about tuna? *Is* / *Are* there any tuna?
   Yes, *there's* / *there are* two cans. *It's* / *They're* next to the bread.
3. Thanks. *Is* / *Are* there any cheese?
   No, sorry. There *isn't* / *aren't* any.
4. Oh well. How about tomatoes? *Is* / *Are* there any tomatoes?
   Yes, *there's* / *there are* some tomatoes in the refrigerator.
5. Great. Thanks. Oh, *is* / *are* there any mayonnaise?
   There's / *There are* two jars of mayonnaise in the refrigerator.
6. Ah, right. Oh, *is* / *are* there any vegetable juice?
   No, there *aren't* / *isn't*, but *there's* / *there are* two cans of apple juice.

B Write. Complete these sentences with *any* or *some*.

1. This is my favorite dish—taco rice. Do you want ____some____?
2. I don't know. Is there _____ meat in it? I don't eat meat.
3. No, there isn't, but there is _____ cheese.
4. Cheese is OK. Is there _____ garlic? I don't like garlic.
5. No, there isn't but there are _____ other spices.
6. Are there _____ tomatoes in it? I love tomatoes.
7. Yes, there are _____ tomatoes in it.
   There are _____ avocadoes in it, too.
8. Mmm. It sounds good. Sure, I want _____.

C Write. What's in your kitchen at home? Answer the questions.

1. Are there any snacks? _____
2. How many bags of cookies are there? _____
3. How much milk is there? _____
4. Are there any chocolates? _____
5. Is there any ice cream? _____

What's for Dinner?

Working on Fluency

A Write. Complete the conversation with sentences from the box below.

> No, that's it. Thanks and see you soon! OK. Buy two packs of mushrooms.
> Great. Are there any mushrooms? Good. Buy about six green peppers.
> Yes. Two packs. Are there any green peppers?

Felix: Hello. OK. I'm at the supermarket.
Becca: _____
Felix: Yes, there are some mushrooms.
Becca: _____
Felix: Wait. Did you say two packs?
Becca: _____
Felix: Green peppers? Yes, there are some green peppers.
Becca: _____
Felix: Hold on. OK. Six green peppers. Anything else?
Becca: _____

B Check [✓]. You need to interrupt the speaker to check or get more information. Check (✓) the best phrase in each pair of sentences.

1. There are four eggs, three sticks of butter, and . . .
   ☐ Hold on. Three sticks of butter, right?   ☐ I'm sorry. There isn't any butter.
2. Please buy some bottles of water and some chips. Also . . .
   ☐ Oh. I like those chips.   ☐ Wait. What kind of chips?
3. Dinner? Well, there are some fajitas in the refrigerator and . . .
   ☐ Excuse me. What are fajitas?   ☐ Sorry. Who?
4. The phone number of the farmers market is 555-1212. Call them and ask . . .
   ☐ Sorry. Is that 555 or 515?   ☐ Excuse me? I hate that place.
5. We need a bag of onions, some carrots, a cabbage, and . . .
   ☐ Oh. I love vegetables!   ☐ Wait. A big bag of onions?

C Match. Draw lines to form pairs of sentences.

1. There aren't any eggs, you know. ○   ○ a. Wait. What restaurant?
2. There's a box of cookies in the kitchen. ○   ○ b. Wait. Black or green?
3. Please buy two bottles of iced tea. ○   ○ c. Excuse me. There are two cartons.
4. There are 40 people in the restaurant and . . . ○ ○ d. Sorry. Where in the kitchen?

20 Unit 4

Critical Thinking

> Think about the reasons people interrupt and polite ways to do it.

A Check [✓]. Check the reason the second speaker interrupts in these conversations.

1. **A:** There isn't any sugar in this cake, but there's some fruit juice.
   B: Sorry. What kind of fruit juice?
   A: Grape juice.
   - ☐ To get more information.
   - ☐ To ask for more time.
   - ☐ To check understanding.
   - ☐ To disagree.

2. **A:** There isn't any butter, but there is some margarine.
   B: Excuse me? There's a stick of butter right here.
   A: Oh, yes. You're right!
   - ☐ To get more information.
   - ☐ To ask for more time.
   - ☐ To check understanding.
   - ☐ To disagree.

3. **A:** OK, first get three eggs, a stick of butter, a jar of honey, and . . .
   B: Wait. I need a pen. I want to take notes.
   A: Sure. Take your time.
   - ☐ To get more information.
   - ☐ To ask for more time.
   - ☐ To check understanding.
   - ☐ To disagree.

4. **A:** OK, that's $87.89. Is there anything else?
   B: Excuse me? $87.89?
   A: Yes, that's right.
   - ☐ To get more information.
   - ☐ To ask for more time.
   - ☐ To check understanding.
   - ☐ To disagree.

B Circle. Look at these ways to interrupt. Circle the phrase that is more polite.

1. Excuse me? / Excuse me. What's that again?
2. I'm sorry. I can't hear you. / Sorry. What?
3. Wait a minute, please. / Wait.
4. Hold on. / Can you hold on please?

C Write. A teacher is speaking. Write sentences to interrupt politely for the following reasons.

1. To get more information.
   Teacher: Please read pages 10–20 for homework.
   You: _____

2. To check understanding.
   Teacher: Next week, class will meet in the library.
   You: _____

3. To ask for more time.
   Teacher: Please be there by 9:00 a.m.
   You: _____

4. To disagree.
   Teacher: I think we have our test on Tuesday.
   You: _____

What's for Dinner? 21

Every Day's a Holiday 5

Working on Vocabulary

A Write. Complete these phrases about holiday activities with the correct verb. Then, write two ideas of your own.

> ~~eat~~   go   send   visit   watch

1. _____eat_____ special food
2. _____ relatives
3. _____ fireworks
4. _____ greeting cards
5. _____ to a restaurant
6. _____
7. _____

B Read and write. Read about Erin's favorite holiday and complete the sentences with words from the box below.

> decorate   watch   wear   ~~is~~   have   eat   sing   give

Hi. I'm Erin and my favorite holiday is St. Patrick's Day. My family ____is____ Irish so it's a special day for us. We always _____ green clothes and we _____ the house with green things, too. In the morning, we always _____ the parade. In the evening, we usually _____ a party at home and we _____ special food. We usually _____ special songs, too. Sometimes my parents _____ all the kids small gifts. It's really a lot of fun.

C Write. When are these holidays? Write the month. Then add two holidays of your own and the month they are in.

Holiday	Month
1. New Year's Day	January
2. Valentine's Day	
3. Halloween	
4. Christmas	
5.	
6.	

Working on Grammar

A Write. How often do you do these things? Rewrite the sentences. Add *always, usually, sometimes,* or *never* to make them true for you.

1. I give friends a present on their birthdays.
   <u>I usually *give friends a present on their birthdays.*</u>
2. I decorate the house for special holidays.
   _____
3. I wear a costume on Halloween.
   _____
4. I spend a lot of money on holiday gifts for my classmates.
   _____
5. My family visits relatives at the beginning of the year.
   _____
6. We eat special food on New Year's Day.
   _____

B Write. Complete these sentences about favorite holiday activities.

1. I always_____.
2. My family usually _____.
3. My classmates sometimes _____.
4. My best friend never_____.

C Circle. Read these sentences and circle the correct preposition.

1. We usually have a party *at /(on)* my birthday.
2. My birthday is *at / on* December 9th.
3. We usually have dinner *on / at* 7 p.m.
4. I always say "Happy New Year!" *on / at* midnight.
5. My family sometimes goes skiing *at / on* winter vacation.
6. We always leave early *at / on* six in the morning.

Every Day's a Holiday

Working on Fluency

A Check [✓]. The second speaker needs to think and wants to use pause fillers. Check the best reply to the questions.

1. What's your favorite holiday?
   - [✓] Hmm, let me see. I really like Christmas.
   - [ ] Oh, I see. I really like Christmas.
2. What do you usually do on Christmas?
   - [ ] Oh well. We usually decorate the house and we exchange presents.
   - [ ] Well, we usually decorate the house and exchange presents.
3. What else do you do?
   - [ ] Maybe. We eat special food and special songs.
   - [ ] Uh. We eat special food and sing special songs.
4. It sounds fun. Is there a party?
   - [ ] Um, not really. It's usually just a few family members.
   - [ ] Yeah, I know. It's usually just family.
5. What special foods do you eat?
   - [ ] Oh, let me see. There are usually Christmas cookies and candies.
   - [ ] Oh really? There are usually Christmas cookies and candies.
6. What's your favorite thing about Christmas?
   - [ ] Hmm. Well, I guess it's the Christmas decorations.
   - [ ] You know. Yes, we decorate the house.

B Number. Number the sentences in the correct order to make a conversation.

a. _____ **Britt:** Hmm. I see. What kind of party?
b. _____ **Mark:** Well, we usually go out to a restaurant or, um, to a karaoke place.
c. __2__ **Britt:** Oh, nothing special usually. How about you?
d. __1__ **Mark:** What do you usually do on the last day of school?
e. _____ **Mark:** Well, I usually have, um, a party with my friends.
f. _____ **Britt:** Karaoke? I love karaoke.
g. _____ **Mark:** Really? You love karaoke? Let's go together.
h. _____ **Britt:** Together? Sure!

Critical Thinking

Think about why people use pause fillers and learn how to use them yourself.

A Read and check [✓]. Read these conversations. Then check the reason why the second speaker probably uses pause fillers.

1. **A:** What time is the flight?
   B: Let's see. It's . . . Oh, here it is. It's at 2:37.
   ☐ Not sure.
   ☐ Needs time to get the next words ready.
   ☐ Needs to remember or figure something out.

2. **A:** When is Saint Patrick's Day?
   B: Maybe . . . in March, I think.
   ☐ Not sure.
   ☐ Needs time to get the next words ready.
   ☐ Needs to remember or figure something out.

3. **A:** What do people do on Earth Day?
   B: They clean things up or, um, what's the word? Recycle.
   ☐ Not sure.
   ☐ Needs time to get the next words ready.
   ☐ Needs to remember or figure something out.

4. **A:** When is the party?
   B: Maybe . . . 7:30? I have to check.
   ☐ Not sure.
   ☐ Needs time to get the next words ready.
   ☐ Needs to remember or figure something out.

B Write. Why do people probably use the *italicized* pause fillers? Write one of the reasons from activity A or an idea of your own.

Pause Filler	Reason
1. Oh, *what's the word?* That's right. Decorate.	_____
2. It's, *you know*, on the 23rd.	_____
3. Well, *I'm not sure but* . . . it's today I think.	_____

C List. List at least two more pause fillers in English. Then write each in a sentence.

Pause Filler	Sentence
You know.	I, um you know, need to check my schedule.
_____	_____
_____	_____

Every Day's a Holiday 25

The Everyday Hero Award 6

Working on Vocabulary

A Number. Match the jobs to the pictures. Write the numbers.

1. a math teacher
2. a school guard
3. a school nurse
4. a cleaning person
5. a cafeteria worker
6. a receptionist

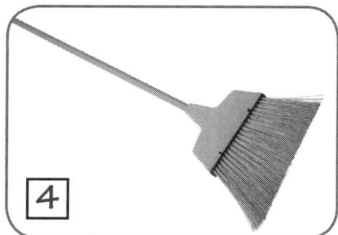 4

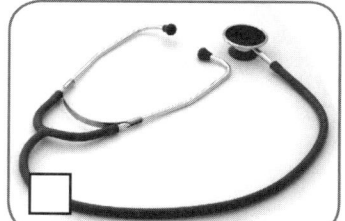

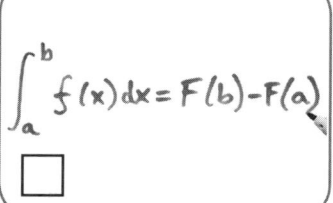

B Write. What do the people above do at their jobs? Complete the sentences.

1. _____A receptionist_____ greets visitors and answers the phone.
2. _____ cooks and serves lunch.
3. _____ works with numbers and students in a classroom.
4. _____ keeps the school building clean.
5. _____ takes care of sick students.
6. _____ keeps everyone safe and guards the school.

C List. Do these adjectives have a positive meaning or a negative meaning? Write them in the correct lists.

nice   terrible   scary   cheerful   strange   friendly   mean   helpful

Positive	Negative

26 Unit 6

Working on Grammar

A Write. Complete the conversations with the correct form of *do* or *be*.

1. **A:** ____Do____ you know Mr. Todd?
   B: ____Is____ he the math teacher?

2. **A:** _____ Mr. Dixon teach math?
   B: No, he _____. He teaches English.

3. **A:** _____ Jenny and Carol the new receptionists?
   B: Yes, they _____. They're really nice.
   A: I agree. They _____ really nice.

4. **A:** _____ that the bus driver?
   B: I think it _____, but I _____ know.
   A: I _____ think he's working.

B Write. Answer these questions with information that is true for you.

1. Is your English teacher from Australia? _____
2. Does your English teacher wear glasses? _____
3. Do you have English class every day? _____
4. Are there a lot of students in your English class? _____
5. Do you have a school cafeteria or snack bar? _____

C Match. Draw lines to match each question to the correct answer.

1. Who makes you laugh? ○
2. Is your sister nice? ○
3. Is she a student, too? ○
4. Does she like her job? ○
5. Who does she work with? ○
6. Do you want to be a nurse, too? ○

○ a. No, I don't. I want to be a doctor.
○ b. My sister does. She's really funny.
○ c. She works with other nurses.
○ d. No, she isn't. She's a nurse.
○ e. Yes, she does. She loves it.
○ f. Yes, she is. I love her a lot.

Working on Fluency

A Check [✓]. Read these conversations and check the best response.

1. This is my brother. He's a photographer.

    ☑ Oh, he sounds interesting.   ☐ Oh, he sounds terrible.

2. Let's have dinner with my friend Sara.

    ☐ She sounds fun.   ☐ That sounds fun.

3. My new boss, Mr. Martin, wears a purple suit every day.

    ☐ He sounds strange.   ☐ He sounds friendly.

4. The lady in the cake shop is my Mom's best friend.

    ☐ That's nice.   ☐ She sounds nice.

5. The school librarian always tells me to be quiet.

    ☐ She sounds mean.   ☐ She sounds friendly.

6. The guy in the snack bar always remembers my name.

    ☐ He sounds nice.   ☐ He sounds fun.

B Write. Respond to these statements with a response similar to the ones in the exercise above or use your own ideas.

1. This is a photo of my brother, Mark. He's a soccer player in Munich.
   He sounds interesting.

2. Mark loves soccer. He even wears his soccer shoes to bed!
   _____

3. Recently, his teammate Claudio took Mark's shoes and laughed at him.
   _____

4. But the other team members are great. They always help Mark a lot.
   _____

5. Yes, I think so too. Hey, let's visit Mark in Munich this summer!
   _____

28 Unit 6

Critical Thinking

Think about how *looks*, *seems*, and *sounds* are used so you can use them better yourself.

A Read and circle. Read the situations and think about how to respond. Circle the verb you think is best.

1. You see a photo of your sister's new boyfriend. He's good looking. He (looks) / sounds great.
2. Your friend invites you to go see a live concert. You want to go. That *looks* / *sounds* fun.
3. Your mother's boss calls her all the time. He calls late at night. That *seems* / *looks* strange.
4. Your roommate orders pizza. You see it and you want some. That *looks* / *sounds* delicious.
5. Your friend tells you about a new restaurant. Dinner costs $300. That *looks* / *seems* expensive.

B Write. Complete the conversations by responding with *looks*, *sounds*, or *seems*.

1. **Petra:** My sister? She doesn't live here. She lives in a tree house.
   Zoe: That _____seems / sounds_____ unusual.
2. **Alex:** This is a photo of my brother's new baby. Her name is Debby.
   Bob: She _____ cute.
3. **Ellen:** I love this computer game. Watch!
   Tim: That _____ fun.
4. **Katie:** Let's go to Tiger Café. They have delicious chocolate cake.
   Jen: That _____ good.

The Everyday Hero Award

Review 2 — Units 4–6

A Write. Read the clues and complete the crossword puzzle.

Across
1. Almost always
4. At this job you have to take care of sick students.
6. A holiday in February
8. A holiday in October
12. The day of your birth
13. Bread and _____
15. The opposite of "never"
16. This office worker greets visitors.
18. Small, dark, red fruit

Down
2. This person guards the school.
3. The opposite of "nice"
5. A word meaning "unusual"
7. The first day of the year
9. This is usually in salads.
10. A popular yellow fruit
11. Another word for "gift"
13. A _____ of water
14. A _____ of rice
17. These are in any omelet.

B Check [✓], draw, and write.
Check *snack*, *main dish*, or *dessert*. Then choose a dish and make a food card. Draw a picture. Explain what's in the dish. Write sentences with *there is* or *there are*.

☐ snack   ☐ main dish   ☐ dessert

Name of dish _____

What's in it?

In this dish there _____

C Number. Sang-mi and Rey are doing the Challenge from Unit 6 in the Student Book. Match these phrases with the phrases in **bold**. Write the numbers.

a. _____ yes, that's right
b. _____ that's her
c. _____ goes to
d. __1__ maybe

e. _____ oh?
f. _____ greets me
g. _____ do you mean the receptionist who works
h. _____ is she the one with

Sang-mi: My award **(1) is for** the receptionist.
Rey: The receptionist. **(2) Does she work** in the main office?
Sang-mi: Yes, **(3) she does**, but I don't know her name.
Rey: So, why her?
Sang-mi: Well, she always smiles and **(4) says hello**.
Rey: **(5) Really?** She sounds friendly.
Sang-mi: Yes, she is very friendly. She always remembers my name too.
Rey: Oh, her! Is she tall?
Sang-mi: **(6) I don't know.** I think she is.
Rey: **(7) Does she have** brown hair?
Sang-mi: **(8) Yes, she does.**

D Research and write. Choose one of these holidays or another of your own. Use the Internet to find information. Then answer the questions. Include a photo or drawing.

☐ Thanksgiving Day   ☐ Cinco de Mayo   ☐ Chinese New Year
☐ Mother's or Father's Day ☐ St. Patrick's Day   ☐ My idea: _____

(Draw or paste picture here.)	What is the name of the holiday?
	When is it?
	Where is it celebrated?
	What do people usually do on this day?
	Other information:

Now Hiring   7

Working on Vocabulary

A Match. Match each job description to the correct job.

1. You have to like animals. ○
2. You have to fly a lot and serve meals. ○
3. You have to take orders and wait on tables. ○
4. You have to use tools and fix engines. ○
5. You have to water flowers and trim trees. ○
6. You have to deliver letters and packages. ○
7. You have to play with children and take care of them. ○
8. You have to wear a uniform and sell roller coaster tickets. ○

○ a. flight attendant
○ b. mail carrier
○ c. kindergarten teacher
○ d. dog trainer
○ e. restaurant server
○ f. gardener
○ g. theme park employee
○ h. car mechanic

B Circle. Find the jobs above in this word search and circle the words.

```
m e h n v f z n e m x q g b m s h s u f c q u t s
j w f b b e w j c t v v j z e x p d u x e w d w r
z c l i z q o r u y h l n z t x k x b a q h s l i
f q i b y g g d p c x a k d f a s w n k a k o o g
p k g b q t t e v h b w m y y g w z n y d q f g j
p k h l i h f q g a r d n e r z p j n n d k v n g
r d t r h q l z g u a b l o j h g w u m g w u f s
r o a x c x e u r e s t a u r a n t s e r v e r p
b g t i l m a i l c a r r i e r s x e v j u k d u
i t t p g q c n t m a c a r m e c h a n i c f k n
b r e r p q b r q l v k o r d e u q q e g i c m j
l a n n r l c c b q r m e s m y e z i b w d v u i
r i d w k i n d e r g a r t e n t e a c h e r b r
m n a z x k s f u x y u q q o m s p p o c n l l g
q e n b h k u h i v y f n o x v q b l r u g q h x
n r t x a t h e m e p a r k e m p l o y e e w c t
o z x g p u o q z q d q l m j c w d f e o e k g m
```

C List. Put jobs from activity A in the correct list. Some jobs may appear on more than one list.

Helps People   flight attendant
Works Outside _____
Fixes Things   _____

32 Unit 7

Working on Grammar

A Read and check [✓]. Read about these jobs. Then complete the chart below.

Office Receptionist
Hours: 9 a.m. to 5 p.m.
Days: Monday – Friday
Uniform: No, but dress nicely.
Duties: greet customers
          send emails

Breakfast Cook
Hours: 5 a.m. to noon
Days: Saturday / Sunday
Uniform: Yes. We buy it.
Duties: cook meals
          clean the kitchen

Office Cleaning Person
Hours: Midnight to 6 a.m.
Days: Monday – Friday
Uniform: Yes. You buy it.
Duties: clean the offices
          open the building at 6 a.m.

	Receptionist	Cook	Cleaning Person
1. You have to use a computer.	✓		
2. You have to work weekends.			
3. You don't have to wear a uniform.			
4. You have to work nights.			
5. You have to talk to customers.			

B Write. What else do you have to do at the jobs above? Write sentences.

Office Receptionist
1. You have to wear something nice.
2. _____

Restaurant Cook
3. _____
4. _____

Office Cleaning Person
5. _____
6. _____

Working on Fluency

A Number. Number the sentences in the correct order to make a conversation.

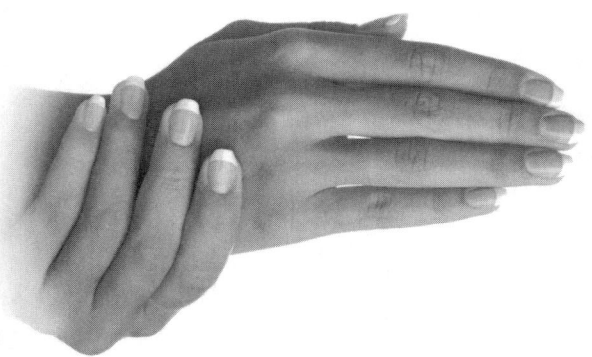

a. _____ Kari: No, I'm not. I'm serious. I'm a hand model.
b. _____ John: A model? You're kidding!
c. _____ Kari: Well, I model rings and gloves.
d. __1__ Kari: I have a new job! I'm a model.
e. _____ John: Rings and gloves? I can't believe it.
f. _____ John: A what? What's a hand model?
g. _____ Kari: It's true. I model rings and gloves.

B Check [✓]. Choose the best response for each statement.

1. **A:** My brother has an interesting job. He's an elephant keeper.
   B: ☐ A what?   ☐ Who?
   A: An elephant keeper. He works at the zoo.

2. **A:** He really likes his job.
   B: What does he do there?
   A: ☐ I can't believe it!   ☐ He has to take care of the elephants.

3. **A:** He has to feed them and exercise them every morning.
   B: ☐ Exercise them? You're kidding.   ☐ A what?
   A: No, I'm serious. He has to take them for a walk.

4. **A:** They go all around the park.
   B: I can't believe it. Really?
   A: ☐ Yes. It's true.   ☐ No, I'm serious!

C Write. Write appropriate responses to complete the conversation.

1. **Phun:** My new job? I'm working for a TV station.
   Kim: _You're joking!_____
   Phun: No, I'm not kidding. I do work in TV.

2. **Phun:** I'm a media coordinator.
   Kim: _____
   Phun: A media coordinator. I have to make schedules for everyone. It's interesting.

Critical Thinking

> Use the information you have and what you know to make good guesses.

A Read and number. Read these job ads. Then match them to the correct job. Write the number.

1. Office Helper
2. Web Designer

☐ Our web design company needs new full-time staff. Do you have computer design skills? Do you have a university degree? Do you like to work hard? Then, send us an email. Experience as designer needed. ASC@cengage.com No phone calls!

☐ Do you have mornings or afternoons free? We need one person M–F from 9 a.m.–noon or 1–5 p.m. You have to answer the phone, make copies, and mail packages. Experience as receptionist needed. Call 444-7777 for more information.

B Write. Write about the jobs in activity A. Write *web designer, office helper, both,* or *no information*.

1. This job is good for a college student.   _____office helper_____
2. You get a lot of money at this job.   _____
3. You have to go to the post office sometimes.   _____
4. You have to use computers at this job.   _____
5. You need an email address to get this job.   _____
6. You have to do many different things at this job. _____
7. You have to have experience.   _____
8. You have to work long hours at this job.   _____

C Write. Think about what web designers and office helpers have to do. Write responses to these questions.

1. What kind of person is an office helper?
   An office helper has to _____
2. What kind of person is a web designer?
   A web designer _____
3. What kind of computer work does a web designer have to do?
   _____
4. What else does an office helper probably have to do?
   _____

Now Hiring

Family Ties 8

Working on Vocabulary

A Unscramble and check [✓]. Unscramble the words. Then check the relatives you have in your family.

1. rehtomrandg _grandmother_ ☐
2. tersis _____ ☐
3. erhtaf _____ ☐
4. ecien _____ ☐
5. ewnehp _____ ☐
6. elcnu _____ ☐
7. tobhrer _____ ☐
8. threom _____ ☐

B Read and write. Who are these people? Write the answers.

1. Your father's sister is your _aunt._
2. Your mother's father's father is your _____
3. Your brother is your father's _____
4. Your aunt is your grandmother's _____
5. Your mother's sister's son is your _____
6. Your brother's wife is your _____
7. Your sister's husband is your _____
8. Your father's father's son is your_____

C Write. Complete the paragraph about Edu's relatives. Use the words in the box.

> ~~ancestors~~   children   husband   married   related   grandmother

These are photos of some of my _ancestors_ in Peru. This is my grandfather's sister, Maria. She was born in Lima in 1923. Next to Maria is her _____ Luis. They _____ in 1944 and they had two _____, Ivonne and Marta. Ivonne has one child, Carlos. Carlos and Maria are _____. Maria is Carlos's _____.

36 Unit 8

Working on Grammar

A Read and match. Draw lines to match the questions and the answers.

1. Who's this?
2. How are you related?
3. When was he born?
4. Is he married?
5. Does he have any children?
6. How old are they?
7. What does your uncle do?
8. Does Michelle have a job?

a. Yes, he is. His wife's name is Michelle.
b. I think he was born in 1962.
c. Yes, he does. Two boys and a girl.
d. He's one of my relatives.
e. He works for a newspaper. He's an editor.
f. He's my Uncle Bob.
g. Yes. She's a flight attendant.
h. They're 14, 11, and 9.

B Number. Each of these sentences gives more information about Bob's family. Write the number of each item in activity A next to the correct piece of information.

_____ They're my cousins.
_____ He's really nice.
_____ She travels a lot.
__1__ He's my father's brother.
_____ His birthday is in July.
_____ They got married in 1990.
_____ He loves his job.
_____ The fourteen-year-old is his wife's daughter.

C Draw and write. Draw a picture of one of your relatives. Then answer the questions.

Your Relative	1. What is this person's name?
	2. How are you related?
	3. When was this person born?
	4. Please tell a little more about your relative.

Family Ties

Working on Fluency

A Write. Complete the conversations using the sentences in the box.

> Sorry? I don't understand.
> Did you say South Wales, New York?
> Did you say "twins"?
> Is that J-U-R-G-E-N?
> I'm sorry. What do you mean "soon"?
> ~~How do you spell your family name?~~

Julie: Hello! What's your name?
Anna: It's Anna Graberhausen.
Julie: _How do you spell your family name?_
Anna: G-R-A-B-E-R-H-A-U-S-E-N.
Julie: Where do you live?
Anna: I live in South Wales, New York.
Julie: _____
Anna: Yes, that's what I said.
Julie: Are you married, Anna?
Anna: Yes, I am. My husband's name is Jurgen.
Julie: _____
Anna: Yes, that's right.
Julie: Do you have any children?
Anna: Well, not now . . . but soon!
Julie: _____
Anna: Oh, I mean I'm pregnant.
Julie: Wow! Is it a boy or a girl?
Anna: Well, it's a boy and a girl.
Julie: _____
Anna: It's twins. You know. Two babies.
Julie: _____
Anna: Yes, I did. Twins.
Julie: How wonderful! Congratulations!

Pregnant

Twins

B Number. Number the sentences from 1 to 9 to make a conversation.

a. ____ **Mr. Bergers:** It's B-E-R-G-E-R-S. I'm from M & T Bank.
b. ____ **Mr. Bergers:** I said M & T Bank.
c. _1_ **Office:** Hello, may I help you?
d. ____ **Office:** No, I'm sorry. You have the wrong number.
e. ____ **Mr. Bergers:** Yes, this is John Bergers.
f. ____ **Office:** Sorry. Is that M as in Martha?
g. ____ **Office:** Please say that again.
h. ____ **Mr. Bergers:** Yes, that's right. M. Anyway, is this Mary Jones?
i. ____ **Office:** Bergers? How do you spell that?

38 Unit 8

Critical Thinking

> Use the information you have to learn more information.

A Read. Read about these families.

My family is small. There's my mom, my dad, my brother, and me. My brother is 12. I'm 19. We have a cat named Max. — Julia

Me? I live with my mother and father, my two sisters, my brother and his wife, and my nephew, Paul. He's cute. — Marcus

My family? I live in an apartment with my sister and my brothers. My brother Aki is 20. My brother Michi is 24. I'm 17. My sister Ayako is 22. Ayako and I study at City College. My dad is a professor there. — Takako

B Check [✓]. Check the statements that you know are true or false using the information you have about Julia, Marcus, and Takako's families.

1. ☐ Julia is a college student.
2. ☑ Julia's brother is probably in junior high school.
3. ☐ Marcus likes his nephew, Paul.
4. ☐ Marcus has a big family.
5. ☐ Marcus lives with his father's mother and father.
6. ☐ Takako and Julia have brothers the same age.
7. ☐ Takako's sister is a student.
8. ☐ Takako and Ayako study English.

C Write. Look at the statements you didn't check in activity B. How can you find the information? Write questions you can ask.

1. _____
2. _____
3. _____

Family Ties 39

Timeline 9

Working on Vocabulary

A Write. Complete each of the phrases below with the correct verb from the box.

> join   buy   have   travel   ~~get~~   write   play   attend   perform

1. __get__ an award
2. _____ a club
3. _____ an accident
4. _____ abroad
5. _____ a newspaper article
6. _____ on stage
7. _____ a car
8. _____ school
9. _____ baseball

B Write. Use the past tense form of the verbs above to complete these stories.

1. When I was in high school, I __performed__ on stage with my friends. It was a lot of fun. I was the singer. I _____ an award for my performance.

2. One day I drove my brother's car to school and _____ a small accident. He was really mad.

3. A few years ago, I _____ a newspaper article about my school. It was really popular so I _____ school and started writing full time.

4. When I was in college, I _____ a sports club. We _____ abroad and I _____ soccer in Germany for a summer.

C Read and number. Each of these sentences finishes one of the stories above. Match each sentence to the correct story and write the number.

____ My friends were surprised, but I love my job now.
____ Europe was a lot of fun. It was great.
____ My brother was angry and I was embarrassed.
__1__ My parents were really proud.

Working on Grammar

A Match and number. Draw lines to make sentences. Then, number the sentences in the correct order to make stories.

____ The show was a hit   a. it was really hard.
____ We practiced every day and   b. so I was really happy.
____ Recently I   c. I joined the ballet club.
_1_ When I was in junior high school   d. performed in the Nutcracker ballet.

____ But then we got lost and   a. I traveled to California with my friends.
____ A few years ago   b. to Redwood Park.
____ The first day   c. we went hiking in the mountains.
____ We drove   d. I was really scared.

____ Last year I   a. a lot every day and every night
____ I practiced   b. bought a guitar and took lessons.
____ I became   c. my CD won the best new CD prize.
____ Recently   d. really good and I recorded a CD.

B Read and write. Use the correct form of the verbs below to complete the paragraph about movie star Angelina Jolie.

> perform   have   move   grow up   meet   win   live   ~~be born~~

Movie star Angelina Jolie **(1)** __was born__ in California in 1975. When she was 2, her family **(2)** _____ to New York and she **(3)** _____ there. When she was 12, she **(4)** _____ in her first movie. In 1999, she **(5)** _____ an Academy Award. A few years ago she **(6)** _____ Brad Pitt. Today, they **(7)** _____ four children and **(8)** _____ together in France.

C Write. Complete the sentences with your own information.

1. When I was in elementary school, _____.
2. When I was in high school, _____.
3. A few years ago, _____.
4. Recently, _____.

Timeline **41**

Working on Fluency

A Check [✓]. Check the best response for each statement.

1. When I was in high school, I went to Disney World.
   ☐ Really? Was it fun?   ☐ Really? Were you sad?
2. In 2005, I designed my own website. It won an award.
   ☐ Wow! Were you scared?   ☐ Wow! Were you surprised?
3. A few years ago I had a terrible traffic accident.
   ☐ Oh! Were you excited?   ☐ Oh! Was anyone hurt?
4. In 2006, I played in a tennis championship—but I lost.
   ☐ Oh. Were you worried?   ☐ Oh. Were you sad?
5. Recently I made a big mistake. I went to the wrong class!
   ☐ Really? Were you embarrassed?   ☐ Really? Were you excited?

B Match. Draw lines to match the statements and responses.

1. Recently I got a new job. ○ ———— ○ a. Hmm. Newspaper delivery. Is it hard?
2. I'm a newspaper delivery person. ○ ○ b. Really? What kind of job?
3. No, but yesterday I made a big mistake. ○ ○ c. Oh well. Don't worry.
4. I delivered a newspaper to the wrong house. ○ ○ d. One newspaper? That's not bad.
5. Maybe not, but my boss was angry. ○ ○ e. A mistake? What do you mean?

C Write. Write appropriate responses to complete the conversation.

Tom: Last year I went to France.
Evan: _____
Tom: No, it wasn't fun. I lost my passport.
Evan: What did you do?
Tom: We went to the police right away.
Evan: _____
Tom: Yes, I was worried! But everything was OK.
      I found it later the same day!

Critical Thinking

Think about appropriate questions and responses.

A Read and number. Read these stories. Then, write the type of story each one is.

sad story   story about danger   funny story

Last year, I joined an outdoor club. Every month we took a trip to someplace in the countryside. In November, we took a trip to the mountains, and I got lost. It started to snow. Then night came and I fell down.

1. _____

I went to London with a tour group. On my first day there, I went shopping at a big department store. Suddenly, a sales clerk said, "May I help you, Yuko?" I said, "Do I know you?" She said, "No. I read your name tag."

2. _____

When I was in high school, my family got a dog. She was so cute. I named her Eclaire and I played with her every day. Well, a few months ago Eclaire got very sick. We took her to the dog hospital.

3. _____

B Read and match. Read these follow-up questions and match each to one of the stories in activity A. Write the number.

_1_ Oh, no! Were you hurt?   ____ Were you cold?
____ Were you worried about her?   ____ Were you sad?
____ Oh! Were you surprised?   ____ Were you embarrassed?

C Read, match, and write. Read and match the correct story from activity A to the sentence that ends it. Then, write an appropriate response.

1. Yesterday, she came home. She's fine now.
   End of Story: _____
   Response: _____
2. We laughed a lot. She gave me her phone number and later we had dinner together.
   End of Story: _____
   Response: _____

Review 3

Units 7–9

A Write. Read the clues and complete the crossword puzzle.

Across
3. Your sister's husband
5. I _____ a cold recently.
7. This person has to fix car engines.
9. Your father's brother's son
10. A person who studies in a school.
13. Your relatives from the past.
14. What soccer players play.
15. _____ a club
16. A birthday is when you were _____.
17. Your father's sister.
18. When you make a mistake, you sometimes feel _____.

Down
1. A ____ has to take care of people.
2. Your mother's father's mother
4. _____ a prize
6. This person has to take care of the house and family.
8. A person who enjoys their job may say it's ____.
10. When something happens quickly without people knowing, it happens _____.
11. When you put on a play, you usually _____ on stage.
12. The past tense of "go"
16. The past tense of "buy"

B Draw and write. Tell about your family. Draw or paste a picture of your family on the left. Then use words below or others to complete the card. Give additional information about each family member. Complete the chart on the following page.

Locations
on the right / left   behind
in front of   in the back / middle / front

Descriptions
nice   friendly   cool
strange   funny   interesting

44 Review 3 • Units 7–9

My Family

This is my family. That's me _____. Next to me, on on the left is _____. He / She is really _____
_____
_____

Sometimes my family is _____, but I think they're _____.

(Draw or paste picture here.)

C Read and number. Diana and Lee are doing the Challenge from Unit 7 in the Student Book. Match these phrases with the phrases in **bold**. Write the numbers.

a. _____ it was great
b. _____ one time
c. _____ you're kidding!
d. _____ awful
e. _____ very
f. _____ won something special
g. _____ in high school
h. __1__ surprisingly won the game

Diana: What's this?
Lee: When I was **(1) a high school student**, I was on the soccer team. **(2) I really loved it.**
Diana: **(3) The soccer team?** Wow! That's cool!
Lee: Yes, it was. But **(4) in one game**, I got hit suddenly in the face with the ball.
Diana: Oh, that's **(5) terrible**. Were you hurt?
Lee: Yes, a little bit, but we **(6) still won**!
Diana: That's great. Were you happy?
Lee: I was **(7) really happy**! I **(8) got an award**.
Diana: What kind of award?
Lee: Best player!

D Research and write. What's your ideal job? Use the Internet to learn about it. Draw or paste a picture of someone doing the job on the card and answer the questions.

My ideal job: _____

1. Where does a person with this job work?
   _____

2. What does a person with this job have to do?
   a. _____
   b. _____
   c. _____

3. How much money does a person with this job make?
   _____

4. Why is this your ideal job?
   _____

(Draw or paste picture here.)

Review 3 • Units 7–9

An Amazing Trip 10

Working on Vocabulary

A Write and check [✓]. Write the words in the correct columns and add one more of your own to each list. Then check the things you like to do when you travel.

- go on a hike
- go dancing in a nightclub
- go to the beach
- go on a picnic
- go to a local restaurant
- go to a shopping mall
- go to a live concert
- go on a boat ride
- go to an amusement park
- go to an art museum

Indoor Activities	Outdoor Activities
☐ _____	☐ _____
☐ _____	☐ _____
☐ _____	☐ _____
☐ _____	☐ _____
☐ _____	☐ _____
☐ _____	☐ _____

B Circle. Circle the word that **cannot** be used with the verb.

1. **take** a trip a vacation a lesson (a shopping)
2. **see** a movie a show a tour a concert
3. **have** dinner a dancing lunch a snack
4. **make** a money a plan a mistake time
5. **buy** souvenirs dinner shopping a train ticket

C Write. Use words from the box to complete this paragraph about a trip to New York.

> dinner   museum   show   souvenirs   stores   ~~tour~~

Welcome to the Big Apple Tours! This morning, you'll take a guided bus ____tour____ of the city. Then we'll go shopping at some department _____ on Fifth Avenue. In the evening, you'll see a _____ on Broadway and have _____ at a famous restaurant. Tomorrow morning, we'll go to the Metropolitan _____ of Art. Then you'll have free time to explore and buy some _____.

46 Unit 10

Working on Grammar

A Write and check [✓]. Complete these tour advertisements with the pronouns and verbs (in parentheses). Use the future form. Then, check the trip you like best.

☐ On this tour (you fly) __you'll fly__ to Orlando, Florida. (You stay) _____ in a resort hotel. On the first day, (you visit) _____ Disney World. On the second day, (you go) _____ to Universal Studios. On the last day, (you have) _____ free time to go shopping or swim in the pool.

☐ On this one-day tour (we travel) _____ to Yosemite National Park. In the morning, (we see) _____ the giant Sequoia trees and in the afternoon, (we visit) _____ Yosemite Valley. In the evening, (we have) _____ a buffet dinner at the world famous Tekoma Lodge.

☐ On the week-long bus tour (you see) _____ the United States. (You begin) _____ your trip in New York and (you finish) _____ your trip in Florida. (We stop) _____ at interesting places and cities each day. (You meet) _____ local people and (they serve) _____ you local food.

B Number. Where do these sentences belong in the tour description below? Write the sentence number.

1. In the afternoon, you'll see a dairy farm.
2. In the morning, you'll visit the kazoo factory.
3. At night, you'll have a campfire.
4. In the evening, you'll have a BBQ dinner.

(kazoo)

Take a one-day tour of my town, Eden, NY! _____ At the factory you'll see how kazoos are made. __1__ On the farm, you'll see cows and chickens. _____ You'll enjoy delicious food and fresh milk. _____ We'll sing songs around the fire. It will be a really great tour!

C Write. Plan a one-day tour of your town or city. Complete the sentences.

Take a one–day tour of my town, _____. In the morning, _____. In the afternoon, _____. In the evening, _____. At night, _____. It will be a really _____ tour!

An Amazing Trip **47**

Working on Fluency

A Check [✓]. Choose the best response.

1. Let's meet in the hotel lobby at 6:00 a.m. Is that OK?
   ☐ Sure! ☐ Oh, nice.
2. Then we'll meet the other members of our group and go to the train station.
   ☐ Right. ☐ Yeah.
3. We have tickets for the train. They're in first class.
   ☐ Oh, nice. ☐ Sure.
4. We'll have breakfast on the train. Do you like Japanese food?
   ☐ Sure. ☐ OK.
5. We'll arrive in Tokyo at 10:30.
   ☐ Uh huh. ☐ Um . . .
6. Then, we'll have a tour of the city.
   ☐ That sounds nice. ☐ Yeah.

B Write. Complete this conversation with appropriate responses from the box.

> Um. No, I don't.   OK. That's fine.
> Really? Thank you!   Sure! What time?

Lim: We'll have the school party at our house this year. Please come!

Kara: _____

Lim: Dinner will be at 7:00. Can you come around 6:00?

Kara: _____

Lim: We'll have a chicken BBQ. You eat meat, right?

Kara: _____

Lim: Well, don't worry. I'll make a special vegetarian dish for you.

Kara: _____

C Write. Think of other ways to respond to each of Lim's statements in activity B. Write a different response for each line.

1. _____ 3. _____
2. _____ 4. _____

48 Unit 10

Critical Thinking

Think about travel preferences and the best kinds of trips for different kinds of travelers.

A Check [✓]. Think about the kind of traveler you are. Check the sentences that fit you. Then add two more statements of your own.

1. ☐ I like to fly or take a train.
   ☐ I like to go by car or bus.
   ☐ I don't care. Anything's OK.

2. ☐ I like to stay in nice hotels.
   ☐ I prefer cheap hotels.
   ☐ I like to do homestays or camp.

3. ☐ I like to take guided tours.
   ☐ I just go. I don't make a plan.
   ☐ I get a map and look on my own.

4. ☐ I like to visit big cities.
   ☐ I want to see small towns or the country.
   ☐ I like to go to unusual places.

5. ☐ I like to travel alone.
   ☐ I like to travel with a tour group.
   ☐ I like to travel with friends or people I meet.

6. ☐ I like to eat in nice restaurants.
   ☐ Cheaper restaurants are OK for me.
   ☐ I like to try food from local stores.

B Read and check [✓]. What kind of traveler are you? What follow-up questions could you ask to get more information?

☐ **The Luxury Traveler** usually stays in very nice hotels and likes to eat in really nice restaurants. This kind of traveler loves cities and is crazy about shopping. The luxury traveler often has expensive suitcases and likes to travel by plane. He or she sometimes likes guided tours.

☐ **The Budget Traveler** is OK with cheap hotels and cheap restaurants or fast food places. This kind of traveler often travels by bus or car and has a backpack or cheap suitcase. The budget traveler likes meeting new people in the countryside or in cities and enjoys taking tours.

☐ **The Adventure Traveler** likes exciting trips. This kind of traveler hates guided tours and often travels alone. He or she travels by bus, plane, train, or car. The adventure traveler loves doing unusual things and meeting new people by doing homestays and shopping at local stores.

An Amazing Trip 49

Computer Dating Service 11

Working on Vocabulary

A Write and check [✓]. Write the words under the correct photos. Then, check the things you are interested in.

> art   computers   fashion   movies   music   reading   ~~sports~~   travel

1. _sports_
2. _____
3. _____
4. _____
5. _____
6. _____
7. _____
8. _____

B Write. Choose two of the things you checked above and complete the sentences with information that's true for you.

Example: I'm interested in sports. For example, I love soccer. My favorite team is Brazil.

1. I'm interested in _____. For example, I love _____.
   _____.

2. I'm also interested in _____. For example, I really like _____.
   _____.

C Write. Write the words that fit you in the *Describes me* list and the ones that don't in the *Doesn't describe me* list. Then add one more word of your own to each list.

> active   athletic   boring   funny   lazy   noisy   outgoing   shy

Describes me: _____
Doesn't describe me: _____

50 Unit 11

Working on Grammar

A Match. Draw lines to make sentences.

1. I like people
2. I don't like
3. I am interested
4. My sister
5. I'm the kind of person
6. My friends

a. wants a partner who is funny and outgoing.
b. who likes to stay home.
c. who are interested in sports.
d. people who are noisy.
e. like people who are honest.
f. in people who play music.

B Read and write. Read about the kinds of people Yoko, Paulo, and Su Hee like. Then complete the sentences about them.

The kinds of people I like . . .
• are interested in sports
• always do their best
—Yoko

The kinds of people I like . . .
• are talkative and funny
• like to go dancing
— Paulo

The kinds of people I like . . .
• are always positive
• don't worry about things
— Su Hee

1. Yoko likes __people who are interested in sports.__
2. She also likes _____
3. Paulo likes _____
4. He also likes _____
5. Su Hee likes _____
6. She also likes _____

C Write and number. Imagine you are at a new school. What kind of friends do you want? Write three sentences. Order them from most (**1**) to least (**3**) important.

Example: __I want friends who are honest.__

1. _____
2. _____
3. _____

Computer Dating Service

Working on Fluency

A Check [✓]. Check the best follow-up question for each statement.

1. I want to go someplace fun.
   - ☐ Like who, for example?
   - ☐ Like where, for example?
2. I like teachers who are funny.
   - ☐ Like who, for example?
   - ☐ Like when, for example?
3. I love Asian food.
   - ☐ Like who, for example?
   - ☐ Like what, for example?
4. I don't like noisy places.
   - ☐ Like who, for example?
   - ☐ Like where, for example?
5. I like some of my brother's friends.
   - ☐ Like who, for example?
   - ☐ Like where, for example?

B Write. Write questions like the ones above to complete the conversation.

Su: I want to eat somewhere special tonight.
Jacob: Like where, for example?
Su: Oh, I don't know, but I love spicy food.
Jacob: _____
Su: Like Thai food. I love Thai food.
Jacob: _____
Su: Tom yum soup. It's great. Hey, I know some good Thai restaurants near here.
Jacob: _____
Su: Thai Gardens. It's on High Street. Let's go after class.
Jacob: _____
Su: How about 5 o'clock?

C Number. Number the sentences in the correct order to make a conversation.

a. ____ **Perry:** Around 6 p.m. Is that OK?
b. _1_ **Perry:** Let's go see a movie sometime.
c. ____ **Perry:** How about tomorrow?
d. ____ **Mari:** Like when, for example?
e. ____ **Mari:** Tomorrow? Around what time?
f. ____ **Mari:** Uh huh. Sounds good!

52 Unit 11

Critical Thinking

Use information to make conclusions.

A Read and number. Read these personal ads. Then match each ad to the correct photo below. Write the ad number.

1. **Love sports?** Me too! I love baseball, soccer, and tennis. I want some friends to play with!
Email me at lovesports@cengage.com

2. **Quiet nights.** I love to watch DVDs and play PC games. I don't like going out very much. Interested?
Email home@cengage.com

3. **Let's chat!** I want some friends who love talking about anything. Let's have coffee or dinner, or chat on the Internet.
Email me at talksalot@cengage.com

4. **Guide me.** From Canada but in New York now. I want to see the city. Can you take me to your favorite places? I love music, movies, and dancing.
Email newintown@cengage.com

Marco _____   Kelly _____   Peter _____   Jennifer _____

B Match and write. Match the statements below to one of the ads in activity A. Write the person's name.

1. __Kelly__ is probably athletic.
2. _____ is probably talkative.
3. _____ probably stays at home a lot.
4. _____ is probably new to the city.
5. _____ is probably not very active.
6. _____ probably likes computers.

C Write. Write one sentence about each person.

Example: __Kelly likes people who are active.__

1. Kelly _____
2. Marco _____
3. Peter _____
4. Jennifer _____

Computer Dating Service 53

Talent Show   12

Working on Vocabulary

A Write and check [✓]. Write the words in the correct columns and add one more of your own to each list. Then, check the things you can do.

> ~~basketball~~   a cake   a card trick   a crossword puzzle
> a funny face   a game of chess   a handstand   homework
> an instrument   a model car   a paper airplane   the violin

Do . . .	Make . . .	Play . . .
☐	☐	☐ basketball
☐	☐	☐
☐	☐	☐
☐	☐	☐
☐	☐	☐

B Circle. Circle the word that **cannot** be used with the verb.

1. play   the piano   (a TV)   the guitar   tennis
2. take   a photo   a bath   a webpage   a bus
3. write   a book   a letter   an email   a picture
4. use   a money   a computer   a cell phone   a dictionary
5. speak   English   Italy   German   Spanish

C Write. Use words from the box to complete this paragraph about how to take a bath.

> fill up   get in   pick out   take off   ~~turn on~~

First, __turn on__ the water and _____ the bathtub. Now, _____ some nice bath salt and put it in the water. Then, _____ your clothes and _____ the tub. Enjoy!

Working on Grammar

A Match. How do you do these things? Draw lines to make sentences.

1. How to send an email
   First, turn on ○
   Now, open your email ○
   Then, click the send button ○

   ○ a. program and write an email.
   ○ b. and send your email.
   ○ c. the computer.

2. How to send a text message
   First, press ○
   Now, choose ○
   Then, type ○

   ○ a. your message and press "send."
   ○ b. the text mail button on your cell phone.
   ○ c. the person you want to text.

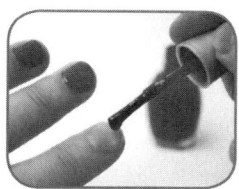

3. How to put on nail polish
   First, take off ○
   Now, choose ○
   Then, let ○

   ○ a. the polish dry. It will take a few minutes.
   ○ b. a new nail polish and put it on your fingernails.
   ○ c. the old nail polish and clean your fingernails.

B Order and write. Number the steps for how to buy a train ticket in the correct order. Then write sentences with *First*, *Now*, and *Then*.

How to Buy a Train Ticket

_____ Take your ticket from the ticket machine.
_____ Find out how much a ticket costs.
_____ Put money in the ticket machine and press the button.

1. _____
2. _____
3. _____

C Write. Think of something you can do. Complete the sentences.

How to _____
1. First, _____
2. Now, _____
3. Then, _____

Working on Fluency

A Check [✓]. Choose the best response.

1. Can you play any musical instruments?
   ☐ Yes, I have.   ☑ No, I can't.

2. Well, let me show you how to play the kazoo.
   ☐ Sorry. No, I don't.   ☐ A kazoo? What's that?

3. It's a kind of musical instrument.
   ☐ Hmm, I see.   ☐ Hmm. You'll see.

4. First, take the kazoo and put it up to your mouth.
   ☐ OK. Now what?   ☐ Oh, nice.

5. Now, put your lips together and hum.
   ☐ Like this?   ☐ Like where, for example?

6. Yes, that's right. Next, hum a song.
   ☐ Oh, this is fun.   ☐ Was it fun?

B Number. Number the sentences from 1–10 to make a conversation.

a. __1__ Sam: Hey, do you know how to play chess?
b. _____ Dina: Like this? Hey, this might be fun!
c. _____ Sam: Sure. I can show you how.
d. _____ Dina: No, I don't. Can you show me?
e. _____ Dina: Great. What should I do first?
f. _____ Dina: Put them on the board like this?
g. _____ Sam: First, put the chess pieces on the board like this.
h. _____ Sam: Yes, that's right. Now, you go first.
i. _____ Sam: Move your pawn like this.
j. _____ Dina: What should I do to go first?

C Write. Write appropriate responses.

1. **Pepe:** Can you speak any foreign languages?
   Gerald: Yes, I can. I can speak English and a little Spanish.
   Pepe: _____

2. **Guy:** Are you interested in learning more Chinese?
   Eunice: Yes, I am. I won a trip to China in a contest!
   Guy: _____

3. **Koby:** Do you have any friends in Brazil?
   Aaron: Yes, I do. My best friend moved there last year.
   Koby: _____

Critical Thinking

> Think about how you learn. Find your learning style.

A Read and check [✓]. Read about visual learners, auditory learners, and tactile learners. Check the type of learner you think you are.

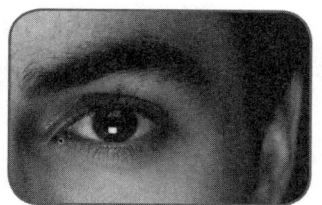
☐ Visual learners learn by seeing. They often sit in the front of the class. This type of learner usually takes notes in class and likes to draw pictures.

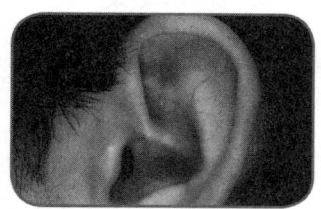
☐ Auditory learners learn by listening and speaking. They like to talk and listen. They usually like to do pair work and group work activities in English class.

☐ Tactile learners learn by doing. This type of learner likes to do projects and activities. They don't like lecture classes. They like dancing and can't sit still for a long time.

B Number. Read the questions and answer with your own information. Circle 4 for *always*, 3 for *sometimes*, 2 for *not really*, and 1 for *never*.

Do you . . .	Always → Never
a) like to do pair work activities in English class? (auditory)	4 3 2 1
b) like to sit in the front of the class? (visual)	4 3 2 1
c) use your hands a lot when you talk? (tactile)	4 3 2 1
d) like to dance? (tactile)	4 3 2 1
e) like to listen to the teacher explain grammar? (auditory)	4 3 2 1
f) like drawing pictures? (visual)	4 3 2 1
g) love sports? (tactile)	4 3 2 1
h) write new words in a notebook? (visual)	4 3 2 1
i) like to listen to stories? (auditory)	4 3 2 1
j) see pictures in your mind when you are reading? (visual)	4 3 2 1
k) usually move your body when you listen to music? (tactile)	4 3 2 1
l) touch your hair or play with your pencil in class? (tactile)	4 3 2 1

C Add. Add your scores in each category (auditory, visual, tactile). What score is highest? That's your learning style. Was your answer in activity A correct?

Review 4 — Units 10–12

A Write. Read the clues and complete the crossword puzzle.

Across
7. The opposite of "positive"
9. Make up you put on your lips
10. A stay with a family is a _____.
15. A museum with paintings is an _____ museum.
16. The opposite of "shy"
17. A _____ bus tour
18. Soccer, basketball, and baseball, for example
19. A _____ house is one that isn't cheap, but also not expensive.

Down
1. _____ dinner
2. Thai food is usually _____.
3. Visiting famous places is called _____.
4. A person who doesn't do much is _____.
5. Pianos, guitars, and violins, for example
6. Magic with cards is a card _____.
8. A meal you eat outdoors is a _____.
11. Another word for "shopping center"
12. Small things people buy to remember a trip
13. _____ a hike
14. A trip by ship

B Draw and write. Make a personal profile. Draw a picture or paste a photograph of yourself on the profile form. Then write.

(Draw or paste picture here.)

Hi Everyone! I'm _____ (name), I'm from _____ (hometown), and I am a _____ (job). I like _____. I am the kind of person who _____. I want friends who are _____ and _____.

Mail me at _____.

C Read and number. Huang and Yoshie are doing the Challenge from Unit 11 in the Student Book. Number these sentences to match the sentences in **bold**.

a. _____ don't show me
b. _____ I understand
c. _____ is this right?
d. _____ choose

e. _1_ yes, I can
f. _____ great
g. _____ don't show you
h. _____ that's right

Huang: Let me show you a card trick. Yoshie, can you help me?
Yoshie: (1) **Sure.** What should I do?
Huang: (2) **Take** a card. Show everyone, but (3) **not me**.
Yoshie: OK. (4) **Got it.** Show everyone, but (5) **not you**.
Huang: (6) **Good.** Now, put the card back.
Yoshie: (7) **Like this?**
Huang: (8) **Yeah.** Next, I do this and this . . . is this the card?
Yoshie: Yes. That's amazing!

D Research and write. What's your ideal city for a vacation? Choose a city. Use the Internet to learn about it. Then plan a three-day trip there. Follow these steps.

1. Find a picture of the city and paste it on the left.
2. Find interesting places to visit. Make a plan for each day in the city.
3. Complete the information.

(Draw or paste picture here.)

City: _____
Where you will stay: _____
Plan
First day: _On the first day_ I will _____
_____
Second day: _____
_____
Third day: _____
_____
Souvenirs you will buy: _____
_____

Review 4 • Units 10–12

Progress Check 1   Units 1–3

A Check [✓]. Choose the word that best completes each sentence and check it. (3 points each)

1. _____ is my new guitar.
   - ☐ a. Those
   - ☐ b. These
   - ☐ c. This
   - ☐ d. The
2. Someday I want to _____ how to speak French.
   - ☐ a. learn
   - ☐ b. go
   - ☐ c. teach
   - ☐ d. see
3. I really _____ movies from the 1950s.
   - ☐ a. crazy about
   - ☐ b. like
   - ☐ c. interesting
   - ☐ d. watching
4. What's your _____ kind of music?
   - ☐ a. best
   - ☐ b. like
   - ☐ c. favorite
   - ☐ d. love
5. There is a convenience store and a park _____ my house.
   - ☐ a. between
   - ☐ b. across
   - ☐ c. next
   - ☐ d. near

B Underline and write. Underline the mistake in the sentence. Then correct it. (4 points each)

Example: What are your favorite song?   What is

1. What is your like time of day?   _____
2. I'm crazy about to play soccer.   _____
3. These is my best friend, Mark.   _____
4. Who is your favorite class at school?   _____
5. There is an Italian restaurant near to my house.   _____

C Check [✓]. Choose the best response to complete each conversation. (3 points each)

1. Hello. I'm Maria Paula De Silva, but please call me Maria.
   - ☐ a. It's nice to meet you, Paula.
   - ☐ b. Who is that?
   - ☐ c. Hi, Maria. It's nice to meet you. I'm Jun.
   - ☐ d. That's interesting.
2. That's Aki. He seems really nice.
   - ☐ a. Oh! It looks nice.
   - ☐ b. Oh really? It's nice.
   - ☐ c. Yes, I think so too.
   - ☐ d. Yes. I am nice.
3. Do you like pop music?
   - ☐ a. It's OK. How about you?
   - ☐ b. Not me, but how about it?
   - ☐ c. Yes, I do. I'm crazy about movies.
   - ☐ d. Really? Why not?
4. I don't like karaoke very much. How about you?
   - ☐ a. Why? It's boring.
   - ☐ b. That's interesting.
   - ☐ c. Not me. I don't like it very much.
   - ☐ d. Oh, really? I don't.
5. There's a small restaurant across from the school. Let's meet there.
   - ☐ a. That seems nice.
   - ☐ b. Oh, really?
   - ☐ c. Across from the school? OK.
   - ☐ d. Yes. It is a small restaurant.

Progress Check 2 — Units 4–6

A Check [✓]. Choose the word that best completes each sentence and check it. (3 points each)

1. There _____ any rice in the kitchen, so please buy some.
   - ☐ a. isn't   ☐ b. aren't   ☐ c. are   ☐ d. is
2. How _____ potatoes are there in the bag?
   - ☐ a. much   ☐ b. many   ☐ c. number   ☐ d. are
3. My birthday is _____ January 20th.
   - ☐ a. at   ☐ b. in   ☐ c. on   ☐ d. during
4. What do you usually _____ on your birthday?
   - ☐ a. do   ☐ b. does   ☐ c. spend   ☐ d. party
5. _____ your English teacher from Australia?
   - ☐ a. Does   ☐ b. Is   ☐ c. Are   ☐ d. Do

B Underline and write. Underline the mistake in the sentence. Then correct it. (4 points each)

1. There are   a box   of cookies   in my room.   _____
2. Is there   any   bags of flour   in the kitchen?   _____
3. My family   always do   something special   on my birthday.   _____
4. Does Mari   working   in the main office   at school?   _____
5. The new   math teacher   always smiles   and say hello.   _____

C Check [✓]. Choose the best response to complete each conversation. (3 points each)

1. I usually invite friends over for a party on the last day of school.
   - ☐ a. That sounds fun.
   - ☐ b. Where do you go?
   - ☐ c. Let's see. Me too.
   - ☐ d. Oh? Where are you?
2. Does Mr. McQueen work in the main office?
   - ☐ a. Yes, he does.
   - ☐ b. Yes, he is.
   - ☐ c. No, he does.
   - ☐ d. No, not me.
3. Is there any whole wheat bread in the kitchen?
   - ☐ a. Yes, there is.
   - ☐ b. Yes, there are.
   - ☐ c. No, but there's some bread.
   - ☐ d. No, there aren't.
4. Is Ms. Frotten a good music teacher?
   - ☐ a. Yes, she does. She's great.
   - ☐ b. No, she doesn't. She teaches math.
   - ☐ c. Yes, she is. She's great.
   - ☐ d. No, she's not my teacher.
5. My brother always helps me with my homework.
   - ☐ a. That sounds strange.
   - ☐ b. He sounds interesting.
   - ☐ c. He sounds nice.
   - ☐ d. That seems fun.

Progress Check 3   Units 7–9

A Check [✓]. Choose the word that best completes each sentence and check it.
(3 points each)

1. My brother _____ a new part-time job.
   - [ ] a. have
   - [ ] b. has
   - [ ] c. does
   - [ ] d. works
2. I always _____ to do a lot of homework.
   - [ ] a. has
   - [ ] b. have
   - [ ] c. must
   - [ ] d. should
3. My Uncle Bob and Aunt Michelle's two children are my _____.
   - [ ] a. brothers
   - [ ] b. nephews
   - [ ] c. cousins
   - [ ] d. parents
4. My father was _____ on July 21st, 1962.
   - [ ] a. born
   - [ ] b. lived
   - [ ] c. died
   - [ ] d. grew up
5. When I was in high school, I _____ to Europe with my family.
   - [ ] a. tripped
   - [ ] b. went
   - [ ] c. vacationed
   - [ ] d. took

B Underline and write. Underline the mistake in the sentence. Then correct it.
(4 points each)

1. At my job I have to serve food and clean tables.   _____
2. Some of my ancestor came from China.   _____
3. My brother is marry with three children.   _____
4. My sister's husband name is Juan.   _____
5. Last years I bought a new guitar and joined a band.   _____

C Check [✓]. Choose the best response to complete each conversation. (3 points each)

1. I make $100 an hour at my new job.
   - [ ] a. You're kidding! That's great!
   - [ ] b. Wow! What do I have to do?
   - [ ] c. A what? I can't believe it.
   - [ ] d. Oh! Yes, you do.
2. Do you have to wear a uniform at your new job?
   - [ ] a. Yes, I do have a new job.
   - [ ] b. My new job? It's great.
   - [ ] c. No, I don't but I have to wear nice clothes.
   - [ ] d. No, he doesn't.
3. One of my relatives is a flight attendant.
   - [ ] a. Oh really? When was she born?
   - [ ] b. Really? How do you spell that?
   - [ ] c. Oh, really? How are you related?
   - [ ] d. Really? I don't believe it.
4. When I was in high school I entered a dance contest and I won first prize.
   - [ ] a. Wow! That's cool.
   - [ ] b. Oh, that's terrible.
   - [ ] c. That's too bad.
   - [ ] d. Wow! Were you scared?
5. Last year, my sister and her husband moved to Hawaii.
   - [ ] a. Hawaii? I'm fine, thank you.
   - [ ] b. Hmm. Were they happy?
   - [ ] c. Yeah.
   - [ ] d. Oh, really? Why?

Progress Check 4   Units 10–12

A Check [✓]. Choose the word that best completes each sentence and check it. (3 points each)

1. A few years ago I went _____ a train trip through Europe.
   - [ ] a. to
   - [ ] b. on
   - [ ] c. in
   - [ ] d. at
2. Next month we _____ fly to Chicago and watch a basketball game.
   - [ ] a. will
   - [ ] b. want
   - [ ] c. go
   - [ ] d. went
3. I'm the kind of _____ who is crazy about sports.
   - [ ] a. people
   - [ ] b. one
   - [ ] c. person
   - [ ] d. ones
4. Can you _____ basketball very well?
   - [ ] a. do
   - [ ] b. make
   - [ ] c. use
   - [ ] d. play
5. I like people _____ don't worry about things.
   - [ ] a. who
   - [ ] b. who's
   - [ ] c. whose
   - [ ] d. they

B Underline and write. Underline the mistake in the sentence. Then correct it. (4 points each)

1. On the first day of our trip we see a bus tour of the city. _____
2. I want a partner's who is outgoing and funny. _____
3. He don't like people who are not honest. _____
4. First, open your phone and pressed the button. _____
5. Now, choose the person you want call. _____

C Check [✓]. Choose the best response to complete each conversation. (3 points each)

1. My best friend and I want to go somewhere fun this summer.
   - [ ] a. Like when, for example?
   - [ ] b. Like what, for example?
   - [ ] c. Like where, for example?
   - [ ] d. Like who, for example?
2. My flight to Sydney will cost $5,000.
   - [ ] a. Oh, that seems cheap.
   - [ ] b. That sounds nice.
   - [ ] c. Wow! That sounds expensive.
   - [ ] d. Sure. That's fine.
3. Are you the kind of person who likes to go out or who likes to stay home?
   - [ ] a. I like to stay home.
   - [ ] b. I'm that kind of person.
   - [ ] c. Not me. How about you?
   - [ ] d. Oh, I really think so.
4. Let me show you something fun. Can you help me?
   - [ ] a. Wow! That is fun.
   - [ ] b. Yes. That's amazing.
   - [ ] c. That sounds fun.
   - [ ] d. Sure. What should I do?
5. Can you play any musical instruments?
   - [ ] a. Sure, I play any.
   - [ ] b. Oh, really? Why?
   - [ ] c. I play piano, but just a little.
   - [ ] d. No, I don't.